Centre for Baptist History a

Occasional Papers Volume 26 a

The Whitley Lec

Holistic Apologetics
Re-Imagining Apologetics for the 21st Century

Seidel Abel Boanerges

Regent's Park College, Oxford

Regent's Park College is a Permanent Private Hall of the University of Oxford.

Copyright © Seidel Abel Boanerges (2025)

Centre for Baptist Studies in Oxford
(formerly the Centre for Baptist History and Heritage)
Regent's Park College, Pusey Street, Oxford OX1 2LB
(Regent's Park College is a Permanent Private Hall of the
University of Oxford)
www.rpc.ox.ac.uk

20 19 18 17 16 15 14 13   7 6 5 4 3 2 1

The right of Seidel Abel Boanerges to be identified as the
Author of this Work has been asserted by them in
accordance with the Copyright, Designs and Patents Act
1988

All rights reserved. No part of this publication may be reproduced, stored in a retrieval system, or transmitted in any form by any means, electronic, mechanical, photocopying, recording or otherwise, without the prior permission of the publisher or a license permitting restricted copying. In the UK such licenses are issued by the Copyright Licensing Agency, 90 Tottenham Court Road, London W1P 9HE.

British Library Cataloguing in Publication Data
A catalogue record for this book is available from the British Library

ISBN 9798309292813

Cover Image: Holistic Apologetics by Dèjì Ayọ̀rìndé, 2025
Used with permission.

Whitley Lecture Dedication

This lecture is dedicated to Dr Alistair McKitterick, Senior Lecturer in Practical Theology at the London School of Theology. Alistair, over the past seventeen years, you have been my lecturer, pastoral tutor, colleague, fellow doctoral student, and most importantly, a dear friend and faithful prayer partner. Your unwavering friendship, wisdom, and support have been a profound blessing, a source of encouragement, and an enduring inspiration in my life and ministry.

Seidel Abel Boanerges
Spurgeon's College, London
Christmas 2024

The Whitley Lecture

The Whitley Lecture was first established in 1949 in honour of W.T. Whitley (1861–1947), the Baptist minister and historian. Following a pastorate in Bridlington, during which he also taught at Rawdon College in Yorkshire, Whitley became the first Principal of the Baptist College of Victoria in Melbourne, Australia, in 1891. This institution was later renamed Whitley College in his honour.

Whitley was a key figure in the formation of the Baptist Historical Society in 1908. He edited its journal, which soon gained an international reputation for the quality of its contents – a reputation it still enjoys nearly a century later as the *Baptist Quarterly*. His *A History of British Baptists* (London: Charles Griffin, 1923) remains an important source of information and comment for contemporary historians. Altogether he made an important contribution to Baptist life and self understanding in Britain and Australia, providing a model of how a pastor-scholar might enrich the life and faith of others.

The establishment of the annual lecture in his name is designed as an encouragement to research and writing by Baptist scholars, and to enable the results of this work to be published. The giving of grants, advice and other forms of support by the Lectureship Committee serves the same purpose. The committee consists of representatives of the British Baptist Colleges, the Baptist Union of Great Britain, BMS World Mission, the Baptist Ministers' Fellowship and the Baptist Historical Society. These organizations also provide financial support for its work.

The Whitley Lectures

Nigel G. Wright, *Power and Discipleship: Towards a Baptist Theology of the State* (1996-97)

Ruth M.B. Gouldbourne, *Reinventing the Wheel: Women and Ministry in English Baptist Life* (1997-98)

Keith G. Jones, *A Shared Meal and a Common Table: Some Reflections on the Lord's Supper and Baptists* (1999)

Anne Dunkley, *Seen and Heard: Reflections on Children and Baptist Tradition* (1999-2000)

Stephen Finamore, *Violence, the Bible and the End of the World* (2001)

Nicholas J. Wood, *Confessing Christ in a Plural World* (2002)

Stephen R. Holmes, *Tradition and Renewal in Baptist Life* (2003)

Andrew Rollinson, *Liberating Ecclesiology: Setting the Church Free to Live Out its Missionary Nature* (2004)

Kate Coleman, *Being Human: A Black British Christian Woman's Perspective* (2006)

Sean Winter, *More Light and Truth?: Biblical Interpretation in Covenantal Perspective* (2007)

Craig Gardiner, *How can we sing the Lord's Song?: Worship in and out of the Church* (2008)

Sally Nelson, *A Thousand Crucifixions: The Materialist Subversion of the Church?* (2009)

David Southall, *The Poetic Paul: On Creating New Realities for Righteousness in Romans* (2010)

E. Anne Clements, *Wrestling with the Word: A Woman reads Scripture* (2011)

Ian M. Randall, *Religious Liberty in Continental Europe: Campaigning by British Baptists, 1840s to 1930s* (2012)

Michael J. Peat, *Answering Mendel's Dwarf: Thinking Theologically about Genetic Selection* (2013)

Helen J. Dare, *Always on the way and in the fray: Reading the Bible as Baptists* (2014)

Ed Kaneen, *What is Biblical 'Ministry'?: Revisiting* diakonia *in the New Testament* (2015)

Joshua T. Searle, *Church Without Walls: Post-Soviet Baptists After the Ukrainian Revolution, 2013–14* (2016)

Richard Pollard, *The Pioneering Evangelicalism of Dan Taylor (1738-1816)* (2017)

Helen Paynter, *Dead and Buried? Attending to the voices of the victim*

in the Old Testament and Today: Towards an ethical reading of the Old Testament texts of violence* (2018)
Joe Kapolyo, *Theology and Culture: An African Perspective* (2019)
Robert Parkinson, *Finding A Friend: The Baptist Encounter with Judaism* (2020)
David McLachlan, *Does This Cross Have Disabled Access? Re-thinking Theologies of Atonement and Disability* (2021)
Andy Goodliff, *The Ruling Christ and the Witnessing Church: Towards a Baptist Political Theology* (2022)
Linda Hopkins, *Learning from Young People's Experiences of Baptist Communion: Re-envisioning the Meal as a Space for Nurturing Faith* (2023)
Tim Judson, *Dark Weeping and Light Sleeping: Whiteness as a Doctrine of De-Formation (2024)*

Foreword

I first met Seidel Abel Boanerges when he served as an associate tutor at Northern Baptist College in Manchester, England, supporting ministers in training in their placements. He has always had a sharp and enquiring theological mind coupled with a heart for the grass roots practice of mission and ministry. I was delighted when he accepted the invitation of the Whitley Committee to be our lecturer for 2025.

Seidel's lecture bears testimony to his wide reading in the field of apologetics and to his concern to help "ordinary Christians" in their day-to-day discipleship. Specifically, he is keen to encourage more people to participate in the Church's apologetic and evangelistic calling. Aware that many Christians are dismissive of classic apologetics for its tendency to rely unduly on mere rational argumentation, Seidel, along with other recent writers in the field, argues for a more holistic approach, one that integrates a variety of ways of defending, explaining and commending the Christian faith. In particular, he suggests that we should welcome the role of spiritual gifts such as prophecy and healing as an important dimension of the apologetic task. This he argues will make our practice more effective, more accessible and more biblical.

If as a church, we turn our back on the commission to give an account of our hope in God then we are failing God and failing the people to whom God sends us. If as a church we imagine that the only way to articulate the faith is through rational argument then we misread the scriptures, misunderstand this generation and misrepresent our Saviour. As Baptists we are of course committed to the priesthood of all believers, but are we also committed to the belief that all believers have a part to play in embodying, enacting and communicating the good news of the kingdom in all its fulness?

I hope that the case put forward by this lecture will stimulate reflection, conversation and action.

Rev Glen Marshall, Chair, Whitley Committee

Holistic Apologetics
Re-Imagining Apologetics for the 21st Century

Introduction

In my experience in Christian ministry and teaching apologetics over the last two decades, one of the most common arguments I have encountered against the practice of apologetics is that it is only for intellectual or clever people. I have come across several church members and even some theological students who are not interested in apologetics, as they perceive themselves to be philosophically inept or too intellectually weak to pursue it. I have heard several responses such as "I like the idea of apologetics, but I cannot argue logically like you, Sir"; "I am not intelligent enough to give a defence of the Christian faith"; or "I do not get all this philosophy, logic, and reasoning stuff, I prefer to stay quiet than confuse others, including myself." I believe these individuals raise a very valid point that should be of concern for Christian apologists today.

I have reviewed several current module descriptors on apologetics from various theological colleges and seminaries on both sides of the Atlantic, and I found that lectures on apologetics often begin with Philosophy 101 topics such as logic, epistemology, reason, or rationality. I acknowledge that philosophical foundations are essential, as sound reasoning helps one to present a persuasive case for the Christian faith with coherence and meaning. However, the disproportionate emphasis placed on philosophical reasoning in apologetics poses a challenge. The traditional definition of apologetics (ἀπολογία) refers to a verbal defence.[1] This restricts apologetic practice to those who can communicate verbally using logic and rationality. What about those who are gifted in nonverbal ways, such as healing, miracles, tongues, music, or drama? This lecture aims to explore nonverbal apologetics in Scripture and contemporary practice.

---

[1] 'ἀπολογία' in *A Greek-English Lexicon of the New Testament and Other Early Christian Literature*, edited by Frederick William Danker (3rd Ed.; Chicago: University of Chicago Press, 2000), 117.

Although apologists often emphasise and encourage an apologetic lifestyle, I wanted to investigate whether different forms of nonverbal apologetics could be actively incorporated and promoted in contemporary apologetics.

A few recent voices have called for a change in the practice of apologetics to incorporate creativity and imagination, developing artistic and action-oriented forms of apologetics. However, the rational, intellectual, and verbal forms still dominate today and have become a barrier for some believers engaging in apologetics. In this paper, I present a case for 'Holistic Apologetics' and argue that a kingdom-focused approach to Christian apologetics provides valuable insights into how contemporary apologetics could be guided towards a new and creative path in our post-Christian society. I present a case for the inclusion of spiritual gifts (healing, tongues, miracles, prophecy, word of wisdom or knowledge, etc.) alongside intellectual apologetics and encourage artistic (literature, painting, drama, music, film) and action-oriented (fighting injustice, solidarity, compassion) forms of apologetics in today's post-Christian society.[2]

This lecture first explores the current practice of apologetics in terms of its meaning and functions and its brief historical development. Secondly, it considers some present challenges of intellectual apologetics and some recent developments that argue for more creativity and imagination in the practice of apologetics today. Thirdly, a case for holistic apologetics is presented based on the theological concepts of the kingdom of God and *missio Dei*.[3] Fourthly, a case for the inclusion of spiritual gifts as apologetics is presented. Finally, the

---

[2] The term "post-Christian" is used in many different ways. In this lecture, a post-Christian society is defined as a Western society where the influence of the Christian faith is in decline, and the influence of secularism is rising. For more details, see, Gene Edward Veith Jr., *Post-Christian: A Guide to Contemporary Thought and Culture* (Wheaton, Ill.: Crossway, 2020).

[3] The concept of Holistic Apologetics was developed as a part of my doctoral studies. Seidel Abel Boanerges, *Homiletical Apologetics and the Local Church: Equipping believers through holistic apologetic preaching*, 2022 [Unpublished doctoral thesis]. University of Chester. <https://chesterrep.openrepository.com/handle/10034/627869>. This doctoral thesis has been accepted for publication by De Gruyter Brill in 2025. Permission has been granted by De Gruyter Brill to use some of that material in this Whitley Lecture.

lecture introduces the reader to the six apologetics styles and the Apologetics Styles Questionnaire,[4] which were developed to encourage the practice of holistic apologetics.[5]

Meaning and Functions of Apologetics

Many years ago, when I encountered the word 'apologetics' in my youth, I thought it was a specialised discipline in how to say a 'sorry'. I was very far from the truth. Later, I realised that the word 'apologetics' is derived from the Greek word 'ἀπολογία' (apologia), meaning 'defence'.[6] Christian Apologetics may be simply defined as the defence of the Christian faith. Originally, 'ἀπολογία' (apologia) was a legal term used in a court of law.[7] In ancient Athens, the defendant was permitted to make a formal verbal defence against the accusation; this was an opportunity to give a 'word back' or to 'speak away' (apo—away, logia—speech) the accusation.[8] Classical Greek works such as Plato's (429–347 BC) *Apology* demonstrate this defence, where Plato defends Socrates (469–399 BC) against his accusers. This same word 'apologia' appears seventeen times in the New Testament in various parts of speech, such as noun form (ἀπολογία [apologia] – 1 Cor. 9:3) or verb form (ἀπολογοῦμαι [apologoumai] – Acts 24:10) to indicate a personal defence against an accusation or the general defence of the gospel.[9]

---

[4] See Appendix One, *Apologetics Styles Questionnaire*, 54-58.
[5] A version of this lecture was presented at the Baptist Scholars International Roundtable (BSIR) organised by Baylor University in 2021. That paper was subsequently published as the following: Seidel Abel Boanerges, 'Kingdom Shaped Apologetics – Making Apologetics Accessible to All', in *Baptists and the Kingdom of God*, edited by T. Laine Scales and João Chaves (Waco, TX: Baylor University Press, 2023), 249-70. Permission has been granted by BUP to use some of that material in this Whitley Lecture.
[6] 'ἀπολογία', 117.
[7] 'ἀπολογία', 117.
[8] J Ramsey Michaels, *1 Peter,* Word Biblical Commentary (Waco, TX: Word Books, 1988), 188.
[9] 'ἀπολογία' in Timothy Friberg and Others (eds.), *Analytical Lexicon of the Greek New Testament* (Grand Rapids, MI: Baker, 2000), 69 and Ken Boa and Robert Bowman Jr., *Faith Has Its Reasons: Integrative Approaches to Defending the Christian Faith* (2nd Ed.; Downers Grove, Ill.: IVP, 2005), 1.

The Christian mandate for apologetics comes from several texts of scripture.[10] It is a biblical command given by Peter to the persecuted Christians that they are to be ready to give a defence for their hope (1 Pet. 3:15); Christians are to contend for their faith (Jude 3); Christians are to eliminate the doubts in the mind of the convert (2 Cor. 10:5); false doctrines and ideas should be addressed (Titus 1:9-11); and God uses reason to argue his case (Isaiah 1:18). Several biblical characters are seen to engage in apologetics in the narratives. For instance, Peter defended the manifestation of tongues in his sermon at Pentecost (Acts 2); Paul reasoned with and persuaded the religious Jews, Stoic and Epicurean philosophers (Acts 17); Stephen defended himself against his accusation of blasphemy in Jerusalem (Acts 6); Jesus through his teaching defended himself against his accusers, presented his identity as Son of Man, Son of God, Messiah, and declared his equality with the Father (Matthew 22:23-33; Mark 2:10-11; Luke 24:39; John 5:17-39). For our discussion, it is helpful to consider the broader context of 1 Pet. 3:15, which is commonly understood as the foundational text for apologetics.[11] The pericope (1 Pet. 3:13-17) is as follows:

> Who is going to harm you if you are eager to do good? But even if you should suffer for what is right, you are blessed. 'Do not fear their threats; do not be frightened. But in your hearts revere Christ as Lord. Always be prepared to give an **answer** to everyone who asks you to give the reason for the hope that you have. But do this with gentleness and respect, keeping a clear conscience, so that those who speak maliciously against your good behaviour in Christ may be ashamed of their slander. For it is better, if it is God's will, to suffer for doing good than for doing evil.

The Greek word 'ἀπολογίαν' (apologian) has been translated as 'answer' in the NIV and KJV versions and as 'defence' in ESV and

---

[10] It can be argued that the whole of Scripture is God's apologetic to humanity.
[11] Many apologists such as Alister McGrath, John Frame and Elaine Graham use this scripture text to discuss the biblical justification for apologetics. See bibliography.

NRSV versions.[12] The difference depends upon the translation philosophy (formal, dynamic, idiomatic or optimal equivalence) employed by a particular version's translation committee.[13] The words 'defence' or 'answer' in context convey meanings such as vindication, rebuttal or explanation. The epistle of 1 Peter was not written to scholars or philosophers but to the believers in the early church.[14] Peter was writing to the church scattered by persecutions throughout Pontus, Cappadocia, Asia and Bithynia.[15] While these new Christians commonly encountered oppression and hostility, Peter advised them not to fear but to stand firm and defend their newfound faith in Christ. James Sire notes, 'it is important to see that the core notion of apologetics—the defence of the Christian faith—is not the focus of this passage'.[16] Davids argues that the aim of the section (3:13-22) was to imitate Christ, 'particularly with reference to their suffering'.[17] Although Sire's broader point is valid, this passage still serves as a helpful text along with other scriptures to understand the discipline of apologetics.

The New Testament does not use the word 'apologia' in a technical sense of a 'formal academic discipline of Christian apologetics', as it is commonly used today.[18] Boa and Bowman Jr. note that the word 'defence' was narrowly used in the first and second centuries to refer to a group of writers known as 'apologists' who, in their works, defended the Christian faith against the accusations.[19] Riecker argues that it was

---

[12] NIV - New International Version; KJV - King James Version; ESV - English Standard Version; NRSV - New Revised Standard Version.
[13] For a helpful resource on Bible translations, please see, Kenneth L. Barker, 'Bible Translation Philosophies' in *The Challenge of Bible Translation: Communicating God's Word to the World*, edited by Glen G. Scorgie and Others (Grand Rapids, MI: Zondervan, 2003), 51-64.
[14] Peter H. Davids, *The First Epistle of Peter,* NICNT (Grand Rapids, MI: Eerdmans, 1990), 7.
[15] Davids, *First Epistle of Peter*, 7.
[16] James Sire, *A Little Primer for Humble Apologetics* (Downers Grove, IL: IVP, 2006), 16.
[17] Davids, *First Epistle of Peter*, 129.
[18] Boa and Bowman Jr., *Faith Has Its Reasons*, 2.
[19] Boa and Bowman Jr., *Faith Has Its Reasons*, 2.

the patristic scholars Fédéric Morel (1552-1630) and Prudent Maran (1683-1762) who introduced the designation of 'apologists' to 'refer to a group of Christian Greek authors in the second century CE'.[20] Two good examples are Justin Martyr's *First Apology, Dialogue with Trypho,* and *Second Apology,* and Tertullian's *Apologeticum*.[21] These early Christian apologists modelled their apologetics on previous Greco-Roman apologetic methodology (such as Plato's *Apology* mentioned above), formally defending the Christian faith against various accusations or misunderstandings.[22] 'It was apparently not until 1794 that apologetics was used to designate a specific theological discipline.'[23]

The Enlightenment compelled apologetics to reinvent itself.[24] Hume rejected revelation and natural theology; Kant rejected traditional proofs (cosmological and ontological arguments) for the existence of God.[25] Darwin advocated a naturalistic explanation for the order and diversity in life.[26] These intellectual challenges prompted modernist apologetics (led by such luminaries as Joseph Butler, William Paley, and Charles Hodge) to embrace reason, evidence and revelation in their apologetic works.[27] McGrath notes that, historically, 'Christian apologists generally responded well to the challenges of rationalism and developed new approaches to apologetics that chimed in with the "spirit of the age"'.[28] Nevertheless, McGrath also observes that such approaches are not helpful to replicate now as each age has its own

---

[20] Siegbert Riecker, *The Old Testament Basis of Christian Apologetics: A Biblical-Theological Survey* (Eugene, OR: Wipf and Stock, 2018), 3.
[21] Boa and Bowman Jr., *Faith Has Its Reasons*, 2.
[22] Boa and Bowman Jr., *Faith Has Its Reasons*, 2.
[23] Boa and Bowman Jr., *Faith Has Its Reasons*, 3.
[24] 'Enlightenment' is a contested term with many different expressions (Descartes, Hume, Kant, Bayle, Spinoza and Toland, etc.) and interpretations (culmination of earlier trends in the Renaissance and Reformation, etc.).
[25] Boa and Bowman Jr., *Faith Has Its Reasons*, 23.
[26] Boa and Bowman Jr., *Faith Has Its Reasons*, 24.
[27] Boa and Bowman Jr., *Faith Has Its Reasons*, 22-24.
[28] Alister E. McGrath, *Bridge-building: Effective Christian Apologetics* (Leicester: IVP, 1992), 28.

issues and concerns.[29] As postmodernity enveloped the West and Western-influenced cultures, it changed the landscape for apologetics once again. Apologetics was again forced to respond to the postmodern values of relativism, religious pluralism, lack of objective truth, anti-foundationalism and the increased emphasis on relationships, communities and personal experience.[30] The change in cultural thinking due to post-Christendom and postmodernism requires the adaptation of apologetics to be culturally relevant.[31]

More recently, in addition to 'defence', scholars have outlined other functions of apologetics, and this section discusses four perspectives from notable apologists (Norman Geisler, Alister McGrath, John Frame and Kenneth Boa & Robert Bowman Jr.). Geisler highlights two essential functions of apologetics: 1) Defence – answering objections; and 2) Offense – answering why only Christianity is true.[32] McGrath emphasises three functions: 1) Defending – identifying the barriers to faith and offering responses; 2) Commending – unpacking the attractiveness of Jesus Christ and his gospel; and 3) Translating – explaining the core ideas of the Christian faith into the cultural vernacular.[33] McGrath does not draw attention to the offensive aspect of apologetics but adds 'commending' and 'translating' as functions. These two scholars approach apologetics from different (modernist and postmodernist) perspectives.[34] McGrath intends to make the Christian faith more plausible and attractive: 'The object of apologetics is not to

---

[29] McGrath, *Bridge-building,* 28.
[30] See, Timothy R. Phillips and Dennis L. Okholm (eds.), *Christian Apologetics in the Postmodern World* (Downers Grove, IL: IVP, 1995).
[31] Stuart Murray defines post-Christendom as 'the culture that emerges as the Christian faith loses coherence within a society that has been definitively shaped by the Christian story and as the institutions that have been developed to express Christian convictions decline in influence.' Stuart Murray, *Post Christendom: Church and Mission in a Strange New World* (Milton Keynes: Paternoster, 2004), 19.
[32] Norman Geisler, "What Is Apologetics and Why Do We Need It?" in *The Harvest Handbook of Apologetics*, ed. by Joseph Holden (Eugene, Ore.: Harvest House, 2018), 22. Original source, Norman Geisler, *Christian Apologetics* (Grand Rapids, MI: Baker, 1976).
[33] McGrath, *Bridge-building,* 17-21.
[34] More about these perspectives will be discussed in the next section.

antagonise or humiliate those outside the church, but to help open their eyes to the reality, reliability, and relevance of the Christian faith', (hence the exclusion of the 'offence' function).[35] From a traditional defence, McGrath's definition moves apologetics towards defence and commendation of the Christian faith. Frame offers a balance between Geisler and McGrath's perspectives. He lists three functions of apologetics: 1) Proof – a rational basis for the Christian faith; 2) Defence – answering objections of unbelief; and 3) Offense – attacking the foolishness of unbelieving thought.[36] He agrees with McGrath's three functions but combines McGrath's 'commending' and 'translating' as one function called 'proof'. He also retains Geisler's 'offence' function, which aims proactively to expose unbelieving thought (2 Cor. 10:4). I personally do not warm to the use of the word 'offence' as it gives the impression that apologists themselves might be offensive. Frame acknowledges this possibility but argues he only uses the term 'as it is used in sports and war: our attack on the enemy'.[37]

Boa and Bowman Jr. refine Frame's three functions and suggest four functions: 1) Vindication or Proof; 2) Defence; 3) Refutation or Offense; and 4) Persuasion.[38] The first three functions are similar to Frame, but the fourth function aims to persuade people to commit their lives to Christ.[39] They argue that 'The apologist's intent is not merely to win an intellectual argument, but to persuade people to commit their lives and eternal futures into the trust of the Son of God who died for them.'[40] It is for this reason that Os Guinness calls apologetics 'pre-evangelism': it prepares the ground for sharing the gospel.[41] Apologetics and evangelism are inextricably linked as the former paves

---

[35] McGrath, *Bridge-building*, 18.
[36] John M. Frame, *Apologetics to the Glory of God: An Introduction* (Phillipsburg, NJ: P&R, 1994), 2.
[37] John M. Frame, *Apologetics: A Justification of Christian Belief* edited by Joseph E. Torres (2nd ED.; Phillipsburg, NJ: P&R, 2015), 189.
[38] Boa and Bowman Jr., *Faith Has Its Reasons*, 4-7.
[39] Boa and Bowman Jr., *Faith Has Its Reasons*, 6.
[40] Boa and Bowman Jr., *Faith Has Its Reasons*, 6.
[41] Os Guinness, *Fool's Talk: Recovering the Art of Christian Persuasion* (Downers Grove, IL: InterVarsity Press, 2015), 110.

the way for the latter, and there is substantial overlap.[42] McGrath discusses this relationship by saying 'apologetics aims to secure consent, evangelism aims to secure commitment', and 'apologetics is conversational, evangelism is invitational'.[43] Boa and Bowman Jr. note the lack of universal agreement about their proposed four functions of Christian apologetics but argue that 'each has been championed by great Christian apologists throughout church history'.[44]

The different functions discussed above are associated historically with different approaches in Christian apologetics. These vary according to doctrinal or theological perspectives. A comprehensive list is presented by Boa and Bowman Jr., who discuss five types of apologetics: 1) Classical Apologetics – which emphasises the use of rational and logical criteria; 2) Evidential Apologetics – which grounds the arguments and the case on empirical and historically verifiable facts; 3) Reformed or Presuppositional Apologetics – presupposes the truth of Christianity (*a priori* commitment) and emphasises the sovereignty of God; and 4) Fideist Apologetics – favours experience and emphasises experiencing truth rather than rational, scientific or historical analysis or evidence.[45] Some interesting correlations can be made between the functions and types of apologetics. Vindication or proof is the focus of classical and evidential apologetics, whereas refutation is the chief aim of reformed apologetics as they presuppose the truth of Christianity. Persuasion is emphasised in fideist apologetics. As Boa and Bowman Jr. note, not everyone agrees with the functions, but all were used

---

[42] It is difficult to give a simple definition for 'Evangelism'. Barrett lists 75 definitions in D. B. Barrett, *Evangelize! A Historical Survey of the Concept* (Birmingham, AL: New Hope, 1987). In this thesis Alvin Reid's definition of evangelism is used which is 'Sharing the good news of Jesus Christ by word and life in the power of the Holy Spirit, so that unbelievers become followers of Jesus Christ in His church and in the culture', Alvin Reid, *Evangelism Handbook - Biblical, Spiritual, Intentional, Missional* (Nashville, TN, B&H, 2009), 31.
[43] McGrath, *Bridge-building,* 21-23.
[44] Boa and Bowman Jr., *Faith Has Its Reasons*, 7.
[45] H. Wayne House, 'What Are Some Apologetic Approaches?', in *The Harvest Handbook of Apologetics*, ed. by Joseph Holden (Eugene, OR: Harvest House, 2018), 37-42; Boa and Bowman Jr., *Faith Has Its Reasons*, 33-45.

effectively in the past. They add a fifth approach to apologetics called 5) Integrative Apologetics, which recognises the value of all approaches and seeks either to integrate them or choose the best approach for the specific individual asking the question.

Over the last three decades, there has been a significant rise in the number of apologetics textbooks published for a postmodern audience. Reviewing these books, I noticed they could be classified into two categories: 1) authors who focus on apologetic communication methods and lifestyle; 2) authors that focus on the content itself where they call for imaginative and creative apologetics. [46] Some address both categories. Apologists such as Stackhouse argue that contemporary apologetics must employ and embrace authenticity, humility, a person-centred approach, and subjective experiences alongside their appeal to evidence and reason.[47] McDowell has edited two books, *A New Kind of Apologist* and *Apologetics for a New Generation*, in which, along with several other scholars, they urge contemporary apologists to note the value of emotions, storytelling, apologetic living, latest technologies, and humbly exploring with the other person the issues of race, justice and environment.[48] McDowell also suggests four characteristics of the new kind of apologist: they are 1) Humble – rather than having an 'I know and I will tell you' attitude, a humble approach is required; 2) Relational – our role is not just conversion but a heart of genuine care for the person; 3) Studious – making time for careful and critical study; and 4) Practitioners – the person's life should reflect the apologetic as authenticity is highly appreciated. [49] More than perhaps even the content, the postmodern influence on apologetics emphasises the communication and exemplary lifestyle of the apologist.

---

[46] More about creative and imaginative apologetics is discussed in section 4.2.

[47] John Stackhouse Jr., *Humble Apologetics: Defending the Faith* (Oxford: Oxford University Press, 2002).

[48] Sean McDowell (ed.), *Apologetics for a New Generation* (Eugene, OR: Harvest House, 2009) and Sean McDowell (ed.), *A New Kind of Apologist* (Eugene, OR: Harvest House, 2016).

[49] Sean McDowell, 'Introduction: A New Kind of Apologist' in *A New Kind of Apologist*, edited by Sean McDowell (Eugene, OR: Harvest House, 2016), 11-20, (15-16).

The Need to Move Beyond Intellectual Apologetics

As mentioned above, the most common argument I have encountered against the practice of apologetics is that it is only for intellectual or 'smart' people. The classical definition of apologetics (ἀπολογία) limits apologetic practice to individuals capable of verbal communication through logic and rationality. But what about those gifted in nonverbal ways, such as healing, performing miracles, speaking in tongues, creating music or art, or engaging in drama? Previously, we noted how the Enlightenment compelled apologetics to reinvent itself, leading to the emergence of modernist apologetics. The rejection of revelation and natural theology by Hume, along with Kant's dismissal of the traditional proofs (cosmological and ontological arguments) for the existence of God, and Darwin's naturalistic explanations for the order and diversity of life, compelled apologists such as Joseph Butler, William Paley, and Charles Hodge to elevate reason, logic, and rationality in their apologetic works. Rational arguments became the trusted tools of that era for asserting truth claims.[50] Modernity confined the Christian faith to the intellectual and cerebral, while passions, emotions, and mystery were often overlooked in academic circles. However, this tendency reduced the gospel to a mere collection of propositional truths and doctrinal statements. Many, including myself, find the modernist apologetic methodologies of contemporary scholars like Norman Geisler, Peter Kreeft, Ronald Tacelli, or William Lane Craig sometimes challenging to practice in some instances. William Lane Craig is a noted apologist, and I benefitted immensely from his apologetic works; sometimes, I find some of his apologetic suggestions too complex. For example, his suggestion of employing Bayes Theorem for calculating the probability of a hypothesis, such as the existence of God or the resurrection of Christ, is too complicated unless the person is a mathematician.[51] I do not dismiss it, as it may serve as a valid apologetic argument for those able to engage at that intellectual level,

---

[50] McGrath, *Mere Apologetics*, 27.

[51] See Figure 1 - William Lane Craig's Citation of Bayes Theorem. William Lane Craig, *Reasonable Faith: Christian Truth and Apologetics*, 3rd edn (Wheaton, IL: Crossway, 2008), 53. Also cited by Elaine Graham, *Apologetics without Apology: Speaking of God in a World Troubled by Religion* (Eugene, OR: Cascade, 2017), 102.

such as Craig. However, it is essential to recognise that this kind of intellectual apologetics does not resonate with everyone in academia or the local church.

$$\Pr(H \mid E) = \frac{\Pr(H) \times \Pr(E \mid H)}{\Pr(H) \times \Pr(E \mid H) + \Pr(\neg H) \times \Pr(E \mid \neg H)}$$

Figure 1 – William Lane Craig's Citation of Bayes Theorem

Several Christian academics and non-academics have observed this issue with modernist apologetics. In *The End of Apologetics*, Myron Penner thinks that apologetics itself 'might be the single biggest threat to genuine Christian faith that we face today'.[52] He believes that 'modern Christian apologetics subtly undermines the very gospel it seeks to defend and does not offer us a good alternative to the skepticism and ultimate meaninglessness of the modern secular condition.'[53] In the 1950s, Martyn Lloyd-Jones prophetically described apologetics as the 'curse of evangelical Christianity' because of its modernistic overemphasis on reason, rationality, and propositions.[54] I could list several other quotes like these, nonetheless, Graham notes this type of modernist apologetics 'resulted in apologetics becoming captive to the very kinds of scientific rationalism that, since the Scientific Revolution, have represented such a serious threat to religion'.[55] Brian McLaren, a leading figure of the emerging church movement, frames his dissatisfaction with traditional, modernist apologetics as implying intellectual warfare rather than friendship.[56]

In the section above, we discussed the purpose and functions of Christian apologetics. If we delve deeper into that purpose, a further

---

[52] Myron Bradley Penner, *The End of Apologetics: Christian Witness in a Postmodern Context* (Grand Rapids, MI: Baker Books, 2013), 12.
[53] Penner, *End of Apologetics*, 49.
[54] Martyn Lloyd-Jones, *Authority* (Edinburgh: Banner of Truth, 1997), 14.
[55] Graham, *Apologetics*, 97.
[56] Brian McLaren, *More Ready Than You Realize: The Power of Everyday Conversations* (Grand Rapids, MI: Zondervan, 2006), 51.

look of the key passage in 1 Peter 3:15 reveals two essential aspects that underpin apologetics: 1) the Lordship of Christ (v15a but in your hearts revere Christ as Lord); and 2) humility in communication (v15b but do this with gentleness and respect). Peter argues that instead of fearing persecution, Christians are to revere Christ. Michaels notes that this reverence is declarative and confessional.[57] Davids goes further and argues that the lordship of Christ is more than just a confession or intellectual commitment to truth. It is a deep commitment to obeying Christ, and this commitment must be visible through our actions.[58] In addition to the lordship of Christ, Christians are to defend their faith with gentleness and respect. Therefore, this pericope implies that apologetics is both seen and heard, done and said. Before a believer attempts to defend their Christian faith, Peter's reminder is that their spiritual condition and moral character are the basis of apologetic communications. McGrath notes that apologetics 'is as much about our personal attitudes and character as it is about our arguments and analysis'.[59] It involves shaping one's character, leaving behind worldly ways and becoming imitators of God (Eph. 5:1) and Christ (Phil. 2: 1–11). For McGrath, apologetics is more than just intellectual and verbal. As a result, non-believers are drawn not only to the reasonableness of the Christian faith but also to the visible transformation of Christ's disciples. Furthermore, new believers are nurtured into devoted disciples by addressing their speech and character. Apologetics evolves into a process through which new believers are taught and equipped to be confident disciples, capable of defending their Christian faith and following Christ in our world faithfully and holistically. Definitions of apologetics such as merely 'rational justification for the truth claims of the Christian faith' are insufficient as they do not incorporate the apologetic lifestyle of a believer associated with defending its truth.[60]

Some Recent Developments in Apologetics

---

[57] Michaels, *1 Peter*, 187.
[58] Davids, *First Epistle of Peter*, 131.
[59] McGrath, *Mere Apologetics*, 18.
[60] Craig, *Reasonable Faith,* 15.

The last three decades have seen a proliferation of apologetic books published for a postmodern audience. Scholars have called for a reform of apologetics to include creativity, imagination, and action. A key publication was the book edited by Andrew Davison, *Imaginative Apologetics*, which calls for more imagination and creativity in apologetics.[61] In that book, Michael Ward's chapter carefully analyses the mutual relationship between reason and imagination and argues that 'imagination is insufficient without reason' and 'imaginative reason is also insufficient'.[62] Alison Milbank and Donna Lazenby argue separately that the visual arts, poetry and literature act as engaging forms of apologetics that 'shock people into engagement with reality'.[63] Lazenby provides several examples from secular literature of how apologists read the 'signs of the times' and engage in culturally relevant apologetics.[64] Instead of proofs, John Hughes calls apologists to focus on the 'inherent beauty and goodness' of the Christian faith, which is in itself attractive and persuasive.[65] Imagination makes people reflect on their existential experiences and maybe reflect on the supernatural. It forces people to think, make parallels and go beyond the routine and accepted ways of thought and practice. Holly Ordway also calls apologists to reimagine Christianity and to recognise that reason, imagination and will are all equally important and should be integrated.[66] She argues that people reject God not because they are 'amoral or apathetic', but because they do not have a proper understanding of God, the Bible, or even sin, and therefore reject the

---

[61] Andrew Davison (ed.), *Imaginative Apologetics: Theology, Philosophy and the Catholic Tradition* (London: SCM, 2011).

[62] Michael Ward, 'The Good Serves the Better and Both the Best: C.S. Lewis on Imagination and Reason in Apologetics', in Davison (ed.), *Imaginative Apologetics*, 59-78 (73 and 75).

[63] Alison Milbank, 'Apologetics and the Imagination: Making Strange' and Donna Lazenby, 'Apologetics, Literature and Worldview', in Davison (eds), *Imaginative Apologetics*, 31-58 (38).

[64] Lazenby, 'Apologetics, Literature and Worldview', 46.

[65] John Hughes, 'Proofs and Arguments', in Davison (ed.), *Imaginative Apologetics*, 3-11 (9).

[66] Holly Ordway, *Apologetics and the Christian Imagination: An Integrated Approach to Defending the Faith* (Steubenville, OH: Emmaus Road, 2017).

Christian faith.[67] People with secular foundations may not engage with a holy God or an incarnate Son, but they do care about 'economic inequality, social justice and racism'.[68] Therefore, we need to reimagine the Christian story to appeal to and persuade people afresh. Paul Gould calls for a holistic approach to apologetics (intellect, imagination, and conscience, or perhaps better truth, goodness and beauty).[69] He argues that apologetics today 'must demonstrate not only the truth of Christianity but also its desirability'.[70] Similar to Lazenby, Gould argues that 'Like the apostle Paul in Athens, we can utilize the cultural narratives embodied in literature, film, music, and art to build bridges to the gospel'.[71] The new apologetics is calling for more imagination, creativity and plausibility through the arts and literature.

An influential voice on this reform is Elaine Graham. She rightly notes that current apologetic practice is inadequate to address a post secular society which is 'both more attuned to, and suspicious of, religious discourse'.[72] Instead of focusing only on rational apologetics, she calls for a balance between word and deed apologetics. Her work is based on that of Kyle Roberts, who asserted that 'apologetics ought to work at integrating not just other disciplines, but also the practices of Christian life and discipleship into and along with the intellectual discourse'.[73] She proposed a 'mission-shaped-apologetics' which grounds apologetics in *missio Dei* and 'requires a three-fold hermeneutic of discernment, participation and witness'.[74] She contends that new apologetics should not overemphasise matters of belief and doctrine but

---

[67] Ordway, *Apologetics and the Christian Imagination*, 60-62.
[68] Ordway, *Apologetics and the Christian Imagination*, 60 and 77.
[69] Paul M. Gould, *Cultural Apologetics Renewing the Christian Voice, Conscience, and Imagination in a Disenchanted World* (Grand Rapids, MI: Zondervan, 2019).
[70] Gould, *Cultural Apologetics*, 25.
[71] Gould, *Cultural Apologetics*, 31.
[72] Graham, *Apologetics*, 71.
[73] Roberts cited in Graham, *Apologetics*, 133-34. The original reference is Kyle Roberts, 'The New Apologetics', 08 February 2011, <https://www.patheos.com/resources/additional-resources/2011/02/new-apologetics-kyle-roberts-02-08-2011> [accessed 21 November 2024].
[74] Graham, *Apologetics*, 125.

rather speak on issues of mission, justice, and social action.[75] In this way, apologetics must 'rest primarily not on arguments that are propositional and doctrinal, but on modes of discourse that are performative, sacramental and incarnational'.[76] When this balance is struck, 'It narrates and renders transparent an entire worldview of loyalties, affections – and, most significantly, everyday practices'.[77] Graham also sees the value of apologetical lifestyle. She calls it 'apologetics of presence' which is partly a retrieval of the kind of apologetics practised by early Christians. She argues that 'exemplary lifestyle is a sign and sacrament of the gospel'.[78] I concur with Graham that apologetics should identify our role in God's mission in this world and fulfil that mission via discernment, participation and witness.[79]

Elaine Graham argues for 'public theology as apologetics'.[80] 'Public theology is the study of the public relevance of religious thought and practice.'[81] In her book, *Between a Rock and a Hard Place* ('rock' referring to the resurgence of religion in the public square and the scepticism towards religion as the 'hard place'), she argues that public theology must be bilingual, rooting itself within the theological language of the church and tradition, and being comprehensible to the non-believers.[82] She argues that 'public theology is not only concerned to do theology about public issues but it is called to do its theology in public'.[83] For Graham, the church is called to 'give an account of the hope' by 'a public vocation of active citizenship' in a 'Performative theology. . . where the language of the church's proclamation to the world is embedded and embodied in its actions'.[84] Based on Gutierrez's

---

[75] Graham, *Apologetics*, 140.
[76] Graham, *Apologetics*, 148.
[77] Graham, *Apologetics*, 8.
[78] Graham, *Apologetics*, 125.
[79] Graham, *Apologetics*, 139.
[80] Elaine Graham, *Between a Rock and a Hard Place: Public Theology in a Post-Secular Age* (London: SCM, 2013), 180.
[81] Graham, *Between a Rock*, 71.
[82] Graham, *Between a Rock*, 99-102.
[83] Graham, *Between a Rock*, 233.
[84] Graham, *Between a Rock*, 222.

work and his liberation theology, Graham argues for an 'Apologetic of Presence' for the 'non-person'.[85] Christians must speak truth to power, advocate for the weak and poor, and challenge every kind of injustice. This then helps us to enact 'the Good News to the poor in a praxis of solidarity, and in speaking truth to power – a public theology validated through the exercise of solidarity, advocacy and prophecy'.[86] 'The primary expression of public theology, then, will be in practical demonstrations that authentic faith leads to transformation.'[87] Although preachers are not the direct audience of Graham's book, this concept is valuable for preachers as they can help their congregations to be better disciples, citizens and 'public theologians' to practice their theology in public.

Graham believes apologetics must diversify from being just an intellectual engagement into more serving and action-oriented forms. I will argue for further reform of the discipline of apologetics to include spiritual gifts as well as creativity and imagination through arts and action (no apologist so far has actively encouraged the use of spiritual gifts as apologetics). I argue below for a more holistic form of apologetics based on the concepts of the kingdom of God and *missio Dei*.

Meaning and Purpose of the Kingdom of God

The Greek word 'βασίλεια' (*basileia*) usually means a kingdom, which is a geographically defined area which is under the power and authority of a ruler.[88] However, the New Testament concept of the 'βασίλεια του Θεού' (*basileia ton theon* - kingdom of God) means a kingdom not bound by earthly geographical limits but is the sphere of God's

---

[85] A non-person is someone who is not fully acknowledged of their rights as a human being. Graham, *Between a Rock*, 216.
[86] Graham, *Between a Rock*, 217.
[87] Graham, *Between a Rock*, 215.
[88] R. T. France, 'Kingdom of God', in *Dictionary for Theological Interpretation of the Bible*, edited by Kevin J. Vanhoozer (Grand Rapids, MI: Baker, 2005), 420-24, (420).

authority and power.[89] The phrase 'kingdom of God', 'his kingdom', or 'your kingdom' is used around seventy times in the synoptic gospels, once in John's gospel and less than twenty times in the rest of the New Testament.[90] The kingdom of God is the eternal, sovereign rule of God over the universe (Psa. 103:19). It is a spiritual reality where God reigns over the lives of those who accept his kingship and worship him. R. T. France argues that the kingdom of God 'is not making a statement about a "thing" called "the kingdom," but about God, that he is king. Thus, "the kingdom of God has come near" means "God is taking over as king," and to "enter the kingdom of God" is to come under his rule, to accept him as king.'[91]

Jesus announced this kingdom has arrived (Matt. 12:28) and inaugurated it in word and deed. France argues that 'Jesus is more than the herald of God's kingship [because] the subject of *basileia* is not God (or "heaven") but the Son of Man (Matt. 13:41; 16:28; 25:31–34; Luke 22:29–30), who now exercises the kingship he came to inaugurate.'[92] Jesus modelled his life and mission around the kingdom. He demonstrated love, mercy, forgiveness, compassion, reconciliation, healing, justice, and solidarity. He formed a kingdom community of disciples and suffered persecution and even death for it. The Sermon on the Mount and Mark 10 contain the revolutionary kingdom values Jesus taught and expected his disciples to demonstrate. In the kingdom, the fruit of the Holy Spirit (love, joy, peace, patience, kindness, goodness, faithfulness, gentleness, and self-control, Gal. 5:22–23) is actualised, and kingdom values must become a way of life for a follower of Christ. The kingdom of God embraces all who trust in Christ regardless of gender, age, ethnicity, education or social status. The disciples followed their master in demonstrating the kingdom's values through sharing the gospel. Jesus taught that his kingdom is not of this world (John 18:36) and that repentance and being born again are necessary to belong to the

---

[89] For a more individualist interpretation, see Scot McKnight, *Kingdom Conspiracy: Returning to the Radical Mission of the Local Church* (Grand Rapids: Brazos Press, 2014), 13.
[90] France, 'Kingdom of God', 420.
[91] France, 'Kingdom of God', 421.
[92] France, 'Kingdom of God', 423.

kingdom (Matt. 4:17 and John 3:3). Although people become part of this kingdom through Christ, this kingdom is not the church. The kingdom is about sovereignty, not the territory. As Boff argues, the kingdom is 'an expression of being or a situation in which justice reigns, mercy is in place, love governs, life triumphs and the feeling of God flourishes in people and in the whole of creation.'[93]

As George Eldon Ladd argued, the kingdom of God is both now and not yet.[94] Much scholarly debate on the kingdom of God is centred on various millennial positions (Premillennialism, Postmillennialism, Amillennialism).[95] The growing interest in millennial studies somewhat distracted from the revolutionary kingdom values to be demonstrated here and now by disciples. Jesus spoke of a kingdom that people will see when it has come with power (Mark 9:1), where Jesus looks forward once again to drinking new wine with his disciples (Mark 14:25). 'This tension between the now and the not yet is illustrated in the traditional form of the Lord's Prayer, which bids us pray "Your kingdom come" and yet concludes with the declaration "Yours is the kingdom."'[96] The kingdom is an eschatological reality that anticipates the future literal rule of Christ on earth (Daniel 2:44, 7:13–14).

As the kingdom is both now and not yet, how are believers to live it out? There are several false dichotomous understandings prevalent in Christian theology. There developed a rift at the beginning of the twentieth century between two Christian traditions, namely a fundamentalist revivalist tradition and a more liberal, social gospel. Goheen argues that this rift was very detrimental to a holistic understanding of the gospel. 'The revivalist tradition emphasized

---

[93] Leonardo Boff, *Global Civilization: Challenges to Christianity and Society* (London: Equinox, 2003), 41.
[94] George Eldon Ladd, *The Presence of the Future: The Eschatology of Biblical Realism*, Reprint edition (Grand Rapids, MI: Eerdmans, 1996).
[95] Discussing these views is beyond the scope of this chapter, but for an excellent comparative study on this topic, see Darrell L. Bock (ed.), *Three Views on the Millennium and Beyond* (Grand Rapids, MI: Zondervan, 1999).
[96] France, 422.

evangelism, while the social gospel tradition stressed sociopolitical action for mercy and justice. Word and deed were torn asunder.'[97] Apologetics has the potential to heal this wound. As Graham argues, the 'focus on mission, and the *missio Dei*, reconnects apologetics with a public, performative understanding of faith. This also represents a move beyond modernity's captivity by neutral, disembodied, cognitive reason, but steps into a world of performative, practical wisdom instead.'[98] I argued above that the mission of Jesus was demonstrated holistically in both word and deed. The concept of *missio Dei* sheds further light on how holistic mission (word and deed) accomplishes God's mission and furthers God's kingdom.

Missio Dei – The Mission of God[99]

Missio comes from the Latin, *'Mittere'*, which means 'to send', and *Dei* is the Latin genitive form for God.[100] Therefore, *missio Dei* means 'the sending of God'. God's mission, the concept of *missio Dei*, is summarised as God's activity to redeem the whole creation (Eph. 1:9-10; Col 1:20). I begin my 'Introduction to Christian Mission' lectures by asking my students to discuss the definitions of mission, missions, evangelism and outreach. The majority of the class (about 80-90%) equate all those four words to 'preaching the gospel to the lost' or 'saving souls'. This demonstrates that vestiges of the missionary era of the 18th and 19th centuries (that viewed mission as something to be done outside of the West and mainly for the conversion of non-Christians) are still prevalent in the church today. The 1952 International Missionary Council in Willingen, Germany set out 'a new theological framework for the mission of the church'.[101] The council demonstrated the scope of mission was to the immediate neighbourhood as well as

---

[97] Michael W. Goheen, *Introducing Christian Mission Today: Scripture, History and Issues* (Downers Grove, IL: IVP Academic, 2014), 228.
[98] Graham, *Apologetics*, 140.
[99] Graham also uses this theological concept to develop her 'mission-shaped apologetics', *Apologetics*, 133-39.
[100] Goheen, *Introducing Christian Mission*, 16.
[101] Goheen, *Introducing Christian Mission*, 75.

every other inhabited area of the world and included social and economic aspects of society. The mission of God was initiated by the Triune God: the Father sending the Son (John 3:16, 4:34, 5:30); both the Father and Son sending the Holy Spirit (John 15:26); and the Father, Son and Holy Spirit sending the church into this world (Matt. 28:19, Mark 16:15, John 20:21). The mission of God is not dependent on humanity, but the church joins the Triune God in his mission to redeem his creation for his glory.

Baptists have demonstrated creativity and imagination in pioneering missional and evangelistic movements throughout history. Baptist distinctives of local church autonomy, individual competency, and the priesthood of all believers all encourage us to be bold in pioneering new forms of ministry and mission in the 21st century. As non-conformists, Baptists have 'a God-given competence to discern the way of Christ for their congregations, and free congregations cannot be compelled into conformity in matters by denominational groups or representatives'.[102] As such, they are free to adopt whatever best practice they see in other denominations. A helpful theology of mission demonstrating the broad scope of missional activity was developed by the Anglican Consultative Council in 1984. What they called the *Five Marks of Mission* were 1) evangelism, 2) discipleship, 3) social action, 4) justice, and 5) environment.[103] Christian mission, they argued, is not only about preaching the gospel or saving souls but also about nurturing new believers, helping the poor, the sick and the needy, challenging violence of every kind, solidarity with the suffering and the poor, fighting for justice and faithful stewardship of God's creation.

A holistic form of apologetics can assist in the five marks of mission mentioned above. The theology of *missio Dei* can serve as the starting

---

[102] Nigel Wright, *Free Church, Free State: A Positive Baptist Vision* (Milton Keynes: Paternoster, 2005), 43.
[103] See Christopher J. H. Wright, *The Mission of God: Unlocking the Bible's Grand Narrative* (Downers Grove, IL: InterVarsity Press, 2006).

point of apologetics to further the kingdom of God. As J Andrew Kirk observes,

> Mission flows from a desire to follow in the way of Jesus, who healed the sick, associated with outsiders, rebuked the self-righteous, challenged the absolute power of the state, restored people's dignity, opposed legalistic and corrupt religious practices, and ultimately gave his life to demonstrate that even enemies encompassed in his love. Jesus tells his disciples to 'go and do likewise'.[104]

From the perspective of holistic apologetics that this thesis is arguing for, the Christian mission is not simply about saving souls for a future kingdom but is about transforming people for the new life of the kingdom of God here until the world is reconciled back to God. This transformational new life is demonstrated by the fruit of the Holy Spirit and in living according to kingdom values. Believers live out the kingdom of God like Jesus in their own local communities. When that happens, churches demonstrate the kingdom of God now and point towards its full realisation then. Searle argues that the kingdom of God is 'the place where the *imagination of God* is expressed in its immense fecundity'.[105] He asserts that 'God interacts with His world on the basis of creative freedom rather than unilateral sovereignty', and therefore we, as his co-workers, must also work creatively towards fulling his *missio Dei* that the kingdom of God might be realised on earth.[106] One of the main functions of practical theology is to explore this imagination.[107] The concept of the kingdom provides opportunities to expand the field of apologetics to include the fruit of the spirit and spiritual gifts alongside intellectual skills, artistic skills and serving

---

[104] J Andrew Kirk, *The Mission of Theology and Theology as Mission* (Valley Forge, PA: Trinity Press International, 1997), 52.
[105] Joshua T. Searle, *Theology After Christendom. Forming Prophets for a Post-Christian World* (Eugene, OR: Cascade, 2018), 123.
[106] Searle, *Theology After Christendom*, 124.
[107] Stephen Pattison, *The Challenge of Practical Theology: Selected Essays* (London: Jessica Kingsley, 2007), 284.

skills. Kingdom-shaped apologetics are beneficial and useful in contemporary society because they integrate the truth of the Gospel with the freedom to create and communicate imaginatively in the power of the Holy Spirit. Rather than reducing mission to either social action or evangelism, a holistic view of mission integrates these aspects together. The Micah Network give a helpful definition of holistic mission:

> Integral [or Holistic] Mission is the proclamation and demonstration of the gospel. It is not simply that evangelism and social involvement are to be done alongside each other. Rather, in integral mission, our proclamation has social consequences as we call people to love and repentance in all areas of life. And our social involvement has evangelistic consequences as we bear witness to the transforming grace of Jesus Christ.[108]

To live according to the kingdom of God means to live and minister like Jesus and his followers in practising holistic mission. Holistic mission, then, includes social justice, healing, prophecy, speaking in tongues, miraculous powers and others listed in 1 Cor. 12:4–11. I develop this aspect of holistic apologetics as part of my broader argument for holistic apologetic preaching.

Spiritual Gifts as Apologetics

Although this view is contested, according to the New Testament, miracles and spiritual gifts are understood as an ongoing blessing to the Church and not confined to an apostolic past.[109] Turner claims that God, through his Holy Spirit, still performs miracles today.[110] The apostle Paul writes that the Holy Spirit blesses the church by giving individual

---

[108] Micah Global, *Definition of Integral Mission*, <https://www.micahnetwork.org/sites/default/files/doc/page/mn_integral_mission_declaration_en.pdf> [accessed on 21 November 2024].

[109] See Craig S. Keener, *Gift & Giver: The Holy Spirit for Today* (Grand Rapids, MI: Baker Academic, 2001).

[110] Max Turner, *The Holy Spirit and Spiritual Gifts: Then and Now* (Carlisle: Paternoster Press, 1996), 20.

believers various spiritual gifts to build up the corporate body of Christ (1 Cor 14:12). A list of spiritual gifts is mentioned in 1 Cor. 12:4–11, namely a message of wisdom, a message of knowledge, faith, healing, miraculous powers, prophecy, distinguishing between spirits, different kinds of tongues, and interpretation of tongues. Some spiritual gifts are not relevant to the non-believer, such as distinguishing between spirits or tongues or interpretation of tongues. However, Paul identifies prophecy as a sign for believers to use that might influence unbelievers who witness its use to believe and worship God, exclaiming 'God is really among you', 1 Cor. 14:25. Two other lists in scripture (Rom. 12:6–8 and 1 Cor. 12:28.) mention further gifts such as serving, teaching, encouraging, giving, leading, showing mercy, helping and guiding, and this implies that no list is exhaustive. For this section, I will focus on the spiritual gifts mentioned in 1 Cor. 12:4–11. The supernatural gifts of healing, messages of wisdom and knowledge, and prophecy (amongst others) have tremendous apologetic potential as they provide evidence and experiences that question materialist presuppositions and can form the basis for encountering the presence of God.[111] For example, Mary Magdalene's account of being a witness to the miraculous resurrection of Jesus would have been an evidential approach to apologetics.

Again, support for this argument to incorporate the spiritual gifts in apologetics can be derived from the pericope of 1 Peter 3:13-17.

> Who is going to harm you if you are eager to do good? But even if you should suffer for what is right, you are blessed. 'Do not fear their threats; do not be frightened. But in your hearts revere Christ as Lord. Always be prepared to give an answer to everyone who asks you to give the reason for the hope that you have. But do this with gentleness and respect, keeping a clear conscience, so that those who speak maliciously against your good behaviour in Christ may be ashamed of their slander. For it is better, if it is

---

[111] Amos Yong, 'The Holy Spirit and the Christian University', Biola University Center for Christian Thought, The Table, 19 May 2012, <https://cct.biola.edu/the-holy-spirit-and-the-christian-university/> [accessed on 15 November 2024].

God's will, to suffer for doing good than for doing evil (NIV).

This epistle was not written to scholars, theologians or philosophers but to believers in the early church.[112] The author of 1 Peter (I shall just refer to 'Peter' for simplicity) wrote to a church scattered by persecution throughout Pontus, Cappadocia, Asia and Bithynia.[113] Earlier, we noted that while the new Christians encountered oppression and hostility, Peter advised them not to fear but to stand firm and defend their newfound faith in Christ. Michaels notes that the word 'defence' or 'answer' used here resembles Paul's usage of the word in Acts 22:1, 24:10, 25:16, where Paul defended himself in front of governors, rulers and a large crowd.[114] Believers are to defend their faith/hope 'παντὶ τῷ αἰτοῦντι' [panti tō aitounti] to anyone who demands in both formal and informal settings as they live for Christ in a pagan culture.[115] Davids notes that although 'defence' can indicate a judicial context, it was mainly used in personal and informal contexts.[116] Forbes argues similarly that 'the use of ἀεὶ [aei] together with παντὶ [panti] supports this less formal setting.'[117]

The majority of believers in the early church would not have trained in rhetoric or philosophy (many of them being slaves or former slaves). Therefore, Peter's instruction to practise apologetics was holistic (both word and deed) for daily life situations in informal contexts, rather than being restricted to public intellectual debate. Although no doubt there were some intellectual believers like Paul who could argue using Greek rhetoric and philosophy, most believers would have used a different kind of defence for their Christian hope such as the use of spiritual gifts of healing or prophecy to demonstrate the power of God. For instance, the blind man in John 9:25 gave a testimonial apologetic of being miraculously healed, saying, 'Whether he is a sinner or not, I don't

---

[112] Davids, *First Epistle of Peter*, 7.
[113] Davids, *First Epistle of Peter*, 7.
[114] Michaels, *1 Peter*, 188.
[115] Michaels, *1 Peter*, 188.
[116] Davids, *First Epistle of Peter*, 131.
[117] Greg W. Forbes, *1 Peter*, EGGNT (Nashville, TN: B&H Academic, 2014), 116.

know. One thing I do know. I was blind, but now I see'.[118] Such apologetics serves as 'pre-evangelism' as it prepares the ground for sharing the gospel. Despite being non-kerygmatic, miraculous signs are a powerful form of apologetics and demonstrate the power of God. My argument, therefore, is for apologetics to open its borders to include the spiritual forms alongside the verbal defence, artistic, serving and exemplary lifestyle.

From a survey of Christian apologists, only a few acknowledged the value of miracles or the supernatural in apologetics (House and Holden, Montgomery, Geisler and Zukeran, and Moreland). House and Holden included the miraculous events of the Old Testament as useful for Christian apologetics today.[119] The examples they suggest include Moses and his miraculous staff (Exo. 4:1-9), the plagues of Egypt (Exo. 7:17-12:30), Elijah on Mount Carmel (1 Kings 18:20-40), and the destruction of Korah (Num. 16:1-35).[120] For House and Holden, therefore, Christian apologetics begins in the Old Testament. John Warwick Montgomery and Norman Geisler included miracles and fulfilled prophecy in their understanding of apologetics.[121] Geisler and Zukeran, in their book, *The Apologetics of Jesus*, argue that Jesus used miracles to authenticate his claim to divinity.[122] They helpfully note that in the Old Testament God validated his spokespeople (Elijah, Moses) through miraculous signs. This understanding was common among the Jewish people in the New Testament. Nicodemus, a member of the Jewish ruling council came to Jesus and said, 'Rabbi, we know that you are a teacher who has come from God. For no one could perform the

---

[118] For various types of apologetics, see Boa and Bowman Jr., *Faith Has Its Reasons*, 33-45.
[119] H. Wayne House and Joseph M. Holden, *Charts of Apologetics and Christian Evidences* (Grand Rapids, MI: Zondervan, 2006), chart, 3.
[120] House and Holden, chart, 3.
[121] John Warwick Montgomery, 'What About a Short History of Apologetics?', in *The Harvest Handbook of Apologetics*, ed. by Joseph Holden (Eugene, OR: Harvest House, 2018), 27-36, (28).
[122] Norman L. Geisler and Patrick Zukeran, *The Apologetics of Jesus: A Caring Approach to Dealing with Doubters* (Grand Rapids, MI: Baker, 2008), 27-46.

signs [miracles] you are doing if God were not with him' (John 3:2).[123] Another example is when John's disciples come to Jesus and ask him,

> Are you the one who is to come, or should we expect someone else?" Jesus replied, "Go back and report to John what you hear and see: The blind receive sight, the lame walk, those who have leprosy are cleansed, the deaf hear, the dead are raised, and the good news is proclaimed to the poor. (Matt 11:3-5).

It can be argued that miracles as a means of apologetics are not something new, but they have always been a part of both the Old and New Testaments. Geisler and Zukeran divide scripture into four periods/ages of miracles – 1) the Mosaic Period, 2) the Prophetic Period (Elijah and Elisha), 3) the Daniel Period (during and after the exile), and 4) the Messiah Period (Jesus).[124] In each of these ages, God authenticated his message through miracles as the author of Hebrews states,

> For since the message spoken through angels was binding, and every violation and disobedience received its just punishment, how shall we escape if we ignore so great a salvation? This salvation, which was first announced by the Lord, was confirmed to us by those who heard him. **God also testified to it by signs, wonders and various miracles, and by gifts of the Holy Spirit distributed according to his will**. (Heb. 2:2-4)

JP Moreland argues that the concept of the kingdom of God 'brings to centre stage the supernatural power of God over disease, death and the kingdom of darkness'.[125] In this kingdom of God, 'power is manifested in healing, demonic deliverance, and divine interaction through dreams,

---

[123] Geisler and Zukeran, *Apologetics of Jesus*, 27.
[124] Geisler and Zukeran, *Apologetics of Jesus*, 27-28.
[125] JP Moreland, *Kingdom Triangle: Recover the Christian Mind, Renovate the Soul, Restore the Spirit's Power* (Grand Rapids, MI: Zondervan, 2007), 173.

visions, words of knowledge/wisdom, and prophetic utterances'.[126] He rightly cautions that, 'As "signs and wonders" continue to increase worldwide, there will be satanic counterfeits'.[127] Despite which theological positions people prefer in terms of spiritual gifts (open but cautious, Third Wave, Pentecostal or Charismatic), Geisler and Zukeran argue that 'Miracles are strong evidence in building a case for Christianity. . . In presenting a case for Christianity, apologists today can utilize this same miraculous evidence'.[128] There is great potential in the spiritual gifts of healing, prophecy, miraculous powers, messages of wisdom and knowledge, and they have to be actively used and encouraged in apologetic practice today.

I conducted field research as a part of my doctoral studies and introduced my participants to the concept of holistic apologetics.[129] Participants in one of the focus groups commented,

> I like the idea of prayer and healing as apologetics as I have never seen it that way. I am not intelligent to explain like you do, but I can certainly pray. I have been a woman of prayer my entire Christian life, and I have seen Jesus heal many people. It is refreshing to know that I am defending my faith by something I can do.[130]

Holistic Apologetics – Re-Imagining Apologetics

Non-verbal forms of apologetics, such as the arts, spiritual gifts, and other expressive methods, should not be considered lesser or less intellectual than other approaches. These various forms of apologetics should be seen as complementary rather than exclusive alternatives. As we have noted in the discussion above, apologetics operates in many ways: rational, intellectual discussions, debates, answered prayer,

---

[126] Moreland, *Kingdom Triangle*, 173.
[127] Moreland, *Kingdom Triangle*, 181.
[128] Geisler and Zukeran, *Apologetics of Jesus*, 40.
[129] See Abel Boanerges, *Homiletical apologetics*.
[130] Abel Boanerges, *Homiletical apologetics*, 176.

miracles, personal testimony, works of art, or even just the power of God's Word. McGrath lists several apologetic pathways that might lead someone to Christ, including intellectual, existential, moral, imaginative and spiritual pathways.[131] Holistic apologetics challenges the practice of some apologists who restrict themselves only to the intellectual and verbal response: decisions to exclude spiritual gifts from doing apologetics are made arbitrarily.[132] Chloe Lynch notes that some evangelicals could have some concerns about imagination as it 'is without moorings, especially in reason and revelation'.[133] She argues that imagination 'makes present that which is otherwise not accessible to us' and 'acts as the source of sense-making, a reordering of the subject(s) of study within a wider set of perspectives upon reality such that new meaning issues from a "shift of perspective"'.[134] In this sense, 'Imagination, therefore, is not opposed to reason or to tradition, to revelation or to experience, insofar as these have revealed the reality of the here-and-now to us'.[135]

A Kingdom of God and *missio Dei* shaped approach to Christian apologetics offers important insights into how contemporary apologetics could be steered to a new and creative path today. Contemporary apologetics must move beyond the intellectual side of apologetics to include and actively encourage to demonstrate the apologetic value of **spiritual apologetics** (healing, miracles and prophecy) alongside **artistic apologetics** (literature, painting, drama and film) and **action-oriented apologetics** (fighting injustice, solidarity, compassion) in our contemporary practice of apologetics. Holistic apologetics does not dismiss traditional intellectual apologetics

---

[131] Alister McGrath, *Intellectuals Don't Need God & Other Modern Myths* (Grand Rapids, MI: Zondervan, 1993), 30-47.
[132] For example, William Lane Craig's book, *Reasonable Faith,* only contains intellectual argument as apologetics.
[133] Chloe Lynch, 'Prophetic Imagination as a Mode of Practical Theology', in *Evangelicals Engaging in Practical Theology: Theology That Impacts Church And World* edited by Helen Morris and Helen Cameron (Abingdon: Routledge, 2022), 40-55 (45).
[134] Lynch, 'Prophetic Imagination', 45.
[135] Lynch, 'Prophetic Imagination', 45.

(moral arguments, proofs, contradictions), but argues that it is only one of the ways to practice apologetics today. If contemporary apologetics is to be effective, it must include and actively encourage the demonstration of spiritual, artistic, and action-oriented apologetics alongside traditional intellectual apologetics.

Now, what is an indicator of the success of this holistic approach to apologetics? The traditional forms of apologetics (verbal and intellectual) can be assessed for their effectiveness in terms of persuasion, refutation, or defence of an argument. Although winning an argument is a step in the right direction, it is not the goal of apologetics. The goal of apologetics is to make "people to commit their lives and eternal futures into the trust of the Son of God who died for them."[136] McGrath discusses this relationship by saying, 'apologetics aims to secure consent, evangelism aims to secure commitment', and 'apologetics is conversational, evangelism is invitational'.[137] If apologetics as 'pre-evangelism' can lead people to that stage of consent through traditional forms such as persuasion, refutation or defence of an argument, or holistic forms which include verbal and intellectual forms and non-verbal forms of apologetics such as serving, literature, healing, messages of wisdom and knowledge, and prophecy, then it is a step in the right direction. Any progress towards helping people commit their lives to Christ would equally be counted as a success based on the Engel's Scale.[138]

I believe that the success of holistic apologetics lies in achieving this goal or even in progressing toward helping people commit their lives to Christ. Secondly, its success can also be measured in participating and fulfilling the various aspects of *missio Dei* such as nurturing new believers; helping the poor, the sick, and the needy; challenging violence of every kind; solidarity with the suffering and the poor; and

---

[136] Boa and Bowman Jr., *Faith Has Its Reasons*, 6.
[137] McGrath, *Intellectuals,* 21-23.
[138] For more details on the Engel's Scale, see, James F. Engel and Wilbert Norton, *What's Gone Wrong with the Harvest? A Communicating Strategy for the Church and World Evangelism* (Grand Rapids, MI: Zondervan, 1975).

fighting for justice and faithful stewardship of God's creation. Both verbal and nonverbal (holistic) forms of apologetics can be used to participate in this mission of God. I understand that the danger of broadening the horizons of any discipline, let alone apologetics, is that it might lose its distinctiveness. It is like the discipline of preaching, which now cannot have a simple definition that captures all of its rich, varied history and the nuances of various contexts and cultures. Swinton and Mowat note, 'the primary task of Practical Theology is not simply to see differently, but to enable that revised vision to create changes in the way that Christians and Christian communities perform the faith'.[139]

In the final focus group of my doctoral field research, participants provided positive feedback regarding holistic apologetics.

> I really like this holistic concept of apologetics as it allows people like me with a passion for social justice to practice apologetics. I want to speak up for the vulnerable and defenceless. I never saw it this way up until now, but I very much like the idea as I am defending and commending my faith that it does not tolerate injustice.[140]

> If we all see Jesus in each other as you said, I think most issues would be resolved in our churches today. I liked the fact that how we treat each other in front of non-believers actually matters. We are living out our faith in front of them. How we behave will either draw them to our faith or push them away from it.[141]

Although the concept of holistic apologetics was very positively received, it remains a theory. I sought something more concrete to translate this theory into practice for local church believers, enabling me to encourage them to practise holistic apologetics within their local communities. Therefore, I designed the Apologetics Styles

---

[139] John Swinton and Harriet Mowat, *Practical Theology and Qualitative Research*, 2nd edn (London: SCM Press, 2016), 255.
[140] Abel Boanerges, *Homiletical apologetics*, 176.
[141] Abel Boanerges, *Homiletical apologetics*, 176.

Questionnaire (ASQ),[142] which was modelled on the evangelism styles questionnaire from the book, *Becoming a Contagious Christian*.[143] In the evangelism styles questionnaire, after answering thirty-six questions by giving points to each question and adding up the score, one can see their strong evangelistic style (Direct, Intellectual, Testimonial, Interpersonal, Invitational, Serving) that best fits/suits them. This is not to box them in that style of evangelism but to show their strengths in the evangelistic activity. Some styles could overlap, or some people might have two strong evangelistic styles rather than just one. I redesigned those thirty-six questions and created six styles of apologetics: Provocative/Polemical, Intellectual, Conversational/Testimonial, Artistic, Charismatic and Action-Oriented.[144] Each style is given a biblical example, a contemporary example, personality characteristics, and a reflective question.

---

[142] I acknowledge the help of my colleague, Dr Chris Sinkinson, in developing this ASQ. See Appendix One for the Apologetics Styles Questionnaire.

[143] Mark Mittelberg, Lee Strobel, and Bill Hybels, *Becoming a Contagious Christian: Communicating Your Faith in a Style That Fits You* (Rev Ed.; Grand Rapids, MI: Zondervan, 2007).

[144] The original ASQ has been improvised and developed in this Whitley Lecture. For the previous ASQ categories, see, Abel Boanerges, 'Kingdom Shaped Apologetics', 267-68.

Type of Apologist	Biblical Example	Contemporary Example	Personality	Reflective Questions
Provocative/ Polemical	Apostle Peter	James White	Confident, direct, and confrontational	Are you sensitive and respectful, or do you sometimes lack tact?
Intellectual	Apostle Paul	William Lane Craig	Logical, inquisitive, enjoys debate and reflection	Do you get stuck on academic matters that can sometimes seem very abstract?
Conversational/ Testimonial	Blind Man (John 9)	Amy Orr-Ewing	Good communicator, open and honest about life	How do you engage people who don't relate to you?
Artistic	King David	Glen Scrivener	Creative, imaginative, thoughtful	Are you clear in what you say, or do people misunderstand?
Charismatic	Prophet Elijah	JP Moreland	Bold, prayerful, impatient, and enthusiastic	Are you sometimes judgmental of others?
Action-Oriented	Dorcas (Acts 9)	Jackie Pullinger	People-centered, social care, boldly fight against injustice	What if people do not see the need for Jesus?

Table 1 – Six Apologetics Styles

Through this Apologetics Styles questionnaire, I was able to encourage people to pursue apologetics who otherwise would not have practised it. I was able to demonstrate that apologetics does not need to be restricted to verbal or cerebral activity, but it can incorporate the diverse creative, artistic, literary, action-oriented and spiritual gifts within a local church. The success of this approach was seen in the numerous testimonies from my students and local church members flooded my office desk that they have explored their apologetic strengths and have created music, drama, creative portraits, images, poems, fiction literature, videos, PowerPoint presentations, puzzles, listening and praying sofas on the high streets, healing on the streets, exercising their spiritual gifts in the public square, and many more. In addition, some have commented on how they have used their spiritual gifts of a message of wisdom or knowledge, and praying in tongues helped them share the gospel with nonbelievers. I believe that holistic apologetics will enable the whole church to perform our faith in participating in the *missio Dei* and furthering the kingdom of God for the glory of God.

Conclusion

This paper presented a case for holistic apologetics and argued for the inclusion of spiritual gifts (healing, tongues, miracles, prophecy, word of wisdom or knowledge, etc.) alongside intellectual apologetics. It encourages artistic (literature, painting, drama, music, film) and action-oriented (fighting injustice, solidarity, compassion) forms of apologetics for today's post-Christian society.

To achieve that aim, this paper first explored the current practice of apologetics in terms of its meaning and functions and its brief historical development. Secondly, it considered some present challenges of intellectual apologetics and some recent developments that argue for more creativity and imagination in the practice of apologetics today. Thirdly, a case for holistic apologetics was presented based on the theological concepts of the kingdom of God and *missio Dei*. Fourthly, a case for the inclusion of spiritual gifts as apologetics was presented and defended. Finally, the paper introduced the reader to the six apologetics styles and the Apologetics Styles Questionnaire, which were developed to encourage the practice of holistic apologetics.

The concept of holistic apologetics presented in this paper may not appeal to everyone. While some may embrace its integration of spiritual gifts, intellectual rigour, artistic expression, and action-oriented approaches as a comprehensive and timely response to a post-Christian society, others may find it too broad or unconventional for their theological framework or apologetic methodology. Additionally, some may question the role of spiritual gifts or artistic forms in apologetic discourse, preferring more traditional or narrowly defined approaches. Still, others might see value in the concept but feel compelled to adapt or develop it further, tailoring it to their specific contexts or convictions. As with any innovative framework, holistic apologetics invites dialogue, critique, and refinement.

I sincerely pray that this holistic apologetics resource will be a blessing to local churches and theological institutions in the UK and across the world, enabling the whole church to perform our faith by participating in the missio Dei and furthering the kingdom of God for the glory and honour of the only wise God, through Jesus Christ, in the power of the Holy Spirit. Amen.

Appendix One

Apologetics Styles Questionnaire

"Becoming the Apologist God Intended You to Be"

Directions: Read each of the 36 statements and place a number that reflects best how well the statement describes you.

That is not like me at all	1
I am a little like that	2
That is somewhat like me	3
I am pretty much like that	4
That is totally me	5

1	In conversations, I like to approach topics directly, without much small talk or "beating around the bush."	
2	I have a hard time getting out of a bookshop without buying a bunch of new books that will help me understand apologetic questions	
3	I often use my personal background or a personal experience in order to illustrate a point I am trying to make.	
4	I relax by listening to music or being creative	
5	I believe supernatural gifts and miracles are important for apologetics today.	
6	I rather give a homeless person some food and clothes rather than talk to them.	
7	I don't have a problem challenging someone when it seems necessary.	

8	I tend to be analytical and logical when I think about a problem.	
9	I am a "people-person" who places a high value on friendship and spends a lot of time with other individuals.	
10	I get frustrated when Christian ministry or a church service is not trying out new ideas or approaches.	
11	I often see answered prayer and want others to know about them!	
12	For me 'gospel in action' is more important than 'gospel in words'.	
13	I do not have a problem confronting my friends with the truth even if it strains the relationship.	
14	In conversations, I like to deal with questions that are holding up a person's understanding.	
15	I tend to draw on my own life experience in order to help someone else with a problem.	
16	I love to be a part of an outreach that does things imaginatively and creatively	
17	I feel God often gives me direct insight (prophecy/word of knowledge) into people's lives.	
18	I see social action as evangelism and apologetics.	
19	I think the world would be a better place if people would stop being so over-sensitive about everything and just tell it like it is!	
20	I enjoy discussions and debates on difficult questions, though I admit I sometimes don't get to the point!	
21	I would rather talk about people and their lives than about ideas.	

22	I don't just listen/watch contemporary forms of art; I spend a lot of time trying to work out what the art is trying to convey.	
23	I am not so bothered about rational arguments, but I am more interested in seeing God at work.	
24	I believe that showing solidarity to a refugee demonstrates that my faith does not give a blind eye to injustice and pain.	
25	I would rather get in trouble for saying too much about judgement than be guilty of saying nothing at all!	
26	I am forever arguing with the TV or radio when I hear people saying things I do not agree with.	
27	I am not embarrassed to share my mistakes and struggles with others when it will help them consider solutions that could help them.	
28	I can express myself in unusual ways, perhaps with photography/dance/painting or writing fiction!	
29	God often prompts me with things to say or answers to give.	
30	I feel like I share the good news of the gospel when I am the hands and feet of Jesus to the poor and marginalised.	
31	Sometimes I am called tactless, but I can't help telling people what I think!	
32	I love to study the logic of the Christian faith and how doctrines hold together.	
33	People generally find it easy to come and talk to me when something is on their mind.	
34	I am often dreaming about plans, visions or just stories in my head!	
35	I think there is a lack of expectation in the church for God to work miracles.	

| 36 | Pursuing the justice of God is furthering the Kingdom of God | |

Transfer the numbers into the grid at the end of the survey and then add up the totals.

The column with the highest number is the character of apologist that may best describe you. You may find that your character is strong in more than one category – that is because you are unique. No one entirely fits a 'neat category'. But once you have done this simple survey, you might look at the examples provided in the box below and find the style of thinkers who best reflect your own interests.

Provocative/ Polemical		Intellectual		Conversation /Testimonial		Artistic/ Creative		Spiritual Gifts		Action- Oriented	
Q1		Q2		Q3		Q4		Q5		Q6	
Q7		Q8		Q9		Q10		Q11		Q12	
Q13		Q14		Q15		Q16		Q17		Q18	
Q19		Q20		Q21		Q22		Q23		Q24	
Q25		Q26		Q27		Q28		Q29		Q30	
Q31		Q32		Q33		Q34		Q35		Q36	
T		T		T		T		T		T	

Use the space below to write down your initial reflections.

Printed in Great Britain
by Amazon